Jeanne Jugan

Foundress of the Little Sisters of the Poor

Paul Milcent

Abridged Third Edition

Translated by the
Little Sisters of the Poor

BY THE SAME AUTHOR

Saint John Eudes. Presentation and Selected Texts.
John S. Burns & Sons.

Jeanne Jugan. Humble, So as to Love More.
Darton, Longman & Todd Ltd., 1980, 230 pages with illustrations.

Paul Milcent was born in Normandy in 1923. He was ordained a priest of
the Eudist Congregation in 1949. After spending some years as a professor
in college, he was assigned to the Formation Program of his Congregation.
Father Milcent served as an advisor to religious communities. He
specialized in the spiritual tradition of Bérulle and Saint John Eudes and
the effect it can have upon the apostolate. Father Milcent died in 2002.

Cover Photo: John Feenan

© Copyright 2012 – Little Sisters of the Poor
www.littlesistersofthepoor.org
ISBN: 978-0-9858898-1-4

Designed by Melissa Halpern-Smith, Advertising Media Plus
Published by Medinger Media Press

Contents

1

A lowly sailor's daughter
∽(1792-1816) ∼

A small thatched cottage with a floor of beaten-earth; a hamlet on the heights overlooking the bay of Cancale in Brittany (France): such was the setting into which Jeanne Jugan was born on October 25, 1792.

1792: the date conjures up dramatic events. Some weeks earlier, two hundred priests had been massacred in Paris because they refused to subscribe to the oath demanded by the revolutionary forces; and a few months later, King Louis XVI would be sent to the guillotine. Already the first stirrings of revolt could be felt, when the West of France would rise to defend its traditions and spark off a bitter civil war, lasting seven or eight years. Like many other churches, that of Cancale would be closed, turned into a fodder-store for troops. These painful events were to set their mark on little Jeanne's childhood.

It would also be affected by the premature death of her father. He was not present when she was born, having gone to sea for several months, for the fishing season. On other occasions, he could not set out, being prevented by his poor health, even though they needed the money he would have earned. And so the mother had to take on some day work as a laundress, to feed the children – eight in all, of whom four died while still young. And then one day, when Jeanne was three and a half, her father set out once more. He never came back. They waited long years for him, but at last were forced to draw the obvious conclusion: he had been lost at sea.

Little Jeanne learned from her mother how to do the everyday household tasks, to look after the cows, how to say her prayers. There

Birthplace of Jeanne Jugan in the hamlet of "Les Petites Croix."

were no longer any organized catechism classes, but many children at this period were secretly catechized by people living near them who had acquired a personal faith and a sense of responsibility as members of a sort of Third Order founded by Saint John Eudes in the seventeenth century. During these difficult years, the members of this Institute lived their lay-women's lives as consecrated to Christ, and played an important role in handing on the Faith. No doubt it was thanks to them that Jeanne learned to read, and that she acquired a clear knowledge of the Christian Faith. Later on, she herself would become a member of this group.

Little Jeanne learned from her mother how to do the everyday household tasks, to look after the cows, how to say her prayers. There were no longer any organized catechism classes, but many children at this period were secretly catechized by people living near them who had acquired a personal faith and a sense of responsibility as members of a sort of Third Order founded by Saint John Eudes in the seventeenth century. During these difficult years, the members of this Institute lived their lay-women's lives as consecrated to Christ, and played an important role in handing on the Faith. No doubt it was thanks to them that Jeanne learned to read, and that she acquired a clear knowledge of the Christian Faith. Later on, she herself would become a member of this group.

Towards the age of fifteen or sixteen, Jeanne was placed as a kitchen-maid, in the service of a neighboring family. Their manor-house, which is still standing, was called La Mettrie-aux-Chouettes.

The young girl arrived there, very timid but willing to learn and to make a success of her new position. Apparently Madame de La Choüe received her very affectionately and treated her very considerately. Down through the years, she held her even in the highest admiration.

La Mettrie-aux-Chouettes, the manor-house where Jeanne worked as a young woman.

For Jeanne was not only employed in the kitchen: she became associated with the family in relieving the poor. She used to visit indigent families or lonely old folk. There she learned about sharing, about respect and tenderness, and also how much tactfulness is necessary if one is not to humiliate those who are in need of help.

It was during her years there that a young man asked her to marry him; according to local custom, she asked him to wait. And she continued her life as a servant, which in her case was also a school of refinement. Some time later, in 1816, a great parish mission was held at Cancale: after the terrible storm of the Revolution, both the Faith and the Church needed to be rebuilt. Jeanne took part in it. It was then that she decided to dedicate herself to the service of God: she would not marry. She made her decision known to the young man.

She knew nothing of what the future held in store. And yet, perhaps, did she have some vague premonition? In any case, she said to her mother one day, "God wants me for Himself. He is keeping me for a work as yet unknown, for a work which is not yet founded."

First steps towards the poor
✥(1817-1823)✥

In 1817, Jeanne, aged twenty-five, left Cancale and her family. Her two sisters were married and would soon be mothers of a family. She herself had made another choice. She left her sisters "everything that was smart or pretty" among her clothes, we are told; and she set off for Saint-Servan to place herself in the service of the poor. She wanted to be poor with them.

And in fact, there was dire misfortune in the town of Saint-Servan. Nearly half the population was inscribed at the Welfare Office, and numerous beggars laid siege to the few families who were better off.

Jeanne took a position as a nurse at the hospital of Le Rosais, which was really too small to accommodate all the unfortunate cases which took refuge there. For a hospital, in those days, was more a refuge for every sort of misery than a center of medical learning; and a nurse's training went no further than was necessary for the preparation of herbal infusions, for doing elementary dressings and applying poultices ...

For about six years, Jeanne attended with devotion the three hundred sick who were crowded in there, together with thirty-five foundling children. Among these poor folk, some suffering from "scurvy, itch and venereal diseases," and with insufficient means at hand, the work was rough and exhausting. Jeanne threw herself into it wholeheartedly. It is related that, over and above, she consecrated her free moments to apostolic initiatives; it was in this way that she took a male nurse aside and taught him the catechism.

She was sustained by a lively faith. During a mission which brought about a great religious revival at Saint-Servan in 1817, congregations aimed at promoting mutual spiritual aid were formed, to stimulate prayer and Christian thinking. Jeanne put her name down for the congregation set up for young women.

A short time later, she became a member of a more exigent group: that same Eudist "Third Order" (or *Society of the Heart of the Admirable Mother*) with which she had come into contact during her childhood through the persons who taught her the catechism.

The women who belonged to this society led a form of religious life at home, and gathered together regularly for communal prayer and sharing. They followed a rule of life and a schedule of daily prayer. Above all else they found therein a strong spiritual tradition, going back to Saint John Eudes: the call to a Christianity of the heart, the invitation to a free and personal faith, a living relationship with Jesus Christ.

Everything in it is based on Baptism, and each year they renewed their baptismal promises. They strove to enter into a communion of thought, of sentiments and of intentions with the Heart of Christ and that of His Mother, which together make but one Heart. "We should always have a small crucifix about our person," said the rule, "we should take it in our hands, kiss it, meditate on it; and He will speak to our hearts … "

The members of this group learned the way of interior freedom, having as its foundation "abnegation of their own will," so as to be able to love in very truth. "A true daughter of the Most Holy Heart of Mary … does not insist on going to church, to religious ceremonies, when her presence is needed elsewhere … of a tender and active charity reaching out wherever it can … they love the poor, the simple, because Jesus Christ and the Blessed Virgin loved them … "

Jeanne belonged to this Third Order for about twenty years, and it would seem that it had a profound influence on her. The spirit of the group can be found in the first rule, or customs, of the Little Sisters of the Poor, especially in its aspects of living communion with Jesus, of renunciation of self, of progress towards interior freedom.

But we left Jeanne back at the hospital of Le Rosais, amongst her poor patients, in dire need of resources. At the end of six years, having overtaxed her strength, Jeanne was utterly exhausted and had to resign her post.

Period of rest and of preparation
❧(1824-1839)❧

J eanne found a new position ready at hand, one which at the same time would be a beneficial respite: a Mademoiselle Lecoq, twenty years her senior and, no doubt, also a member of the Third Order, took her in not only as a servant but as a friend. During twelve years, these two women lived a common life to the rhythm of prayer, household tasks, visits to the poor, and catechism lessons to children. They attended daily Mass, read spiritual books to each other; they talked freely about God.

Mademoiselle Lecoq, watchful for the health of her companion, obliged her to take things easy, and took care of her.

Together with the people around them, they lived through good times and hard times. And there were times too of real hardship, in particular the years 1825-1832: as a consequence of a serious economic crisis in London in 1825, and of poor potato crops in France during several consecutive years, many folks knew real hunger. The number of beggars was on the increase, and men out of work were to be seen roving in bands throughout the countryside. At Saint-Servan the list of unfortunates became ever longer. The two friends were aware of all this, and played a generous part in the collective efforts designed to relieve those in distress.

But dear Mademoiselle Lecoq fell ill and, in June 1835, she died. She bequeathed to Jeanne her furniture and a small sum of money.

To gain her livelihood, Jeanne set about working on a daily basis for some families of Saint-Servan who called on her help: housework, laundry, caring for the sick. Bonds of friendship were struck in this manner with quite a few persons; later on these relationships were very precious for Jeanne and for those with whom she was about to link her destiny.

Jeanne made friends with a woman much older than herself, named Françoise Aubert, or Fanchon. Pooling their resources, they rented an apartment in the heart of Saint-Servan: two rooms on the second floor and another two rooms in a loft above[1]. There the two friends lived a life to the rhythm of prayer, almost the same as that which Jeanne had led with Mademoiselle Lecoq. Franchon did spinning at home; Jeanne continued to work by the day, outside.

The small oratory in their Saint-Servan apartment where Jeanne and her first companions prayed. Eventually Jeanne slept in this loft area, having given her bed on the first floor to Anne Chauvin.

But soon a third person came to join them: a young girl of seventeen, an orphan, called Virginie Trédaniel. She seems to have had no problem in entering the prayerful life of her two seniors. From 1838, all three of them – aged seventy-two, forty-six and seventeen – were to lead a regular common life, which only death was to interrupt.

Jeanne was more and more attentive to the needs of the poor folk who surrounded her at Saint-Servan, but what was to be done? She felt powerless in the face of such immense and varied needs. But was it enough to be wounded to the heart? Shouldn't she allow herself to be wounded in her flesh as well? Should she not, in a kind of madness, even share the necessities of life, even share her home? Wouldn't that be really loving?

It was this very step that Jeanne was about to take, and she was never to look back.

[1] This house is still in existence and has become a place of pilgrimage.

4

Jeanne gives up her bed

❧(1839-1842)❧

Towards the end of 1839, possibly in the first cold days of winter, Jeanne came to a decision: with Fanchon's and Virginie's approval, Jeanne brought an old woman home with her, Anne Chauvin (the widow Haneau) who was blind and infirm. Until then, the latter had been assisted by her sister, but the sister had fallen ill and had been taken to the hospital. It was a desperate case.

It is related that to get her up the narrow stairs of the house, Jeanne carried her on her back. What is certain is that she gave her own bed and herself moved up into the loft. And she "adopts her as her mother."

Shortly afterwards another old woman, Isabelle Coeuru, joined Anne Chauvin. She had served her old masters to the end: these having fallen on hard times, she had spent all her own savings on them and then had gone out begging to keep them alive. When they died, she was left worn out and infirm. Jeanne heard this impressive story of faithfulness and sharing, and straight away, without delay, she received her into their dwelling. This time, Virginie was the one to give up her bed and move into the loft.

At night, having made their two patients comfortable and said goodnight to honest Fanchon, Jeanne and Virginie would climb up the ladder leading to their loft and, taking off their shoes so as not to make any noise, would finish off their work and say their prayers before going to bed.

All three of them worked (Virginie was a dressmaker) to feed and

Spiral staircase up which Jeanne carried her first Resident, Anne Chauvin, as she welcomed her into her home.

support five people, two of whom were old and sick; sometimes they had to stay up late at night to do the mending or the washing. Perhaps it may date from this time that Jeanne had recourse to those families she had come to know well.

Virginie had a friend of about the same age as herself, called Marie Jamet, who very soon became acquainted with Jeanne and her household. She herself lived with her parents, and worked with her mother, who kept a small shop.

Marie came often to visit her friend, and she too came to have an affection for Jeanne and to hold her in admiration. And all three of them – and sometimes Fanchon as well – would talk of God, of the poor, and of the questions which life presented. Jeanne told her two young friends about her membership in the Eudist Third Order. They were too young to join it themselves but, with Jeanne's help, they drew up a little rule of life, inspired by that of the Third Order.

Marie and Virginie spoke of their friendship, and the spiritual help received and given, to a young curate of Saint-Servan, the Abbé Auguste Le Pailleur, who was their confessor. He encouraged them, and promised to help them.

He made Jeanne's acquaintance, and began to take an interest in the group and its charitable activities. Enterprising, ingenious and able, he also was concerned about the poor; he thought it right for him to support a work which could very well grow into something bigger. His support was certainly to be efficacious, but also the source of how many tribulations!

On October 15, 1840, with his help, the three friends formed a charitable association which adopted for its statutes that little rule worked out by Marie and Virginie.

This group would soon include a new member. A young working-woman of twenty-seven, very sick, was taken in by Jeanne. She thought she was going to die – but she recovered, and from then on she too participated in this common enterprise. Her name was Madeleine Bourges.

And so it came about that, around these two old ladies sheltered by Jeanne, a small cell formed: it was already the embryo of a large Congregation, to be known much later as the Little Sisters of the Poor.

In 1840, Jeanne and her companions did not know this. But, already, they dreamt of succouring other needs, of offering comfort, security and tenderness to other folk as well. As for money, God would not let them down. But the house was full: they decided to move elsewhere.

A lease was available on a former bar situated close by: it was a huge, low room, with two smaller rooms adjoining. The price was one hundred francs a year. They accepted the bargain, and moved in at Michaelmas 1841. They labeled the dwelling the "Big Basement," a name which has come down over the years.

Twelve elderly women, including those already received, took possession of it. Jeanne, Fanchon and Virginie occupied one of the small

View of the sea from the House of the Cross, Saint-Servan.

rooms at the end. Marie and Madeleine brought their aid, and a little money. And the old ladies, as much as they could, used to spin wool or hemp: the results of their handiwork were sold and that too was a help for the upkeep of the group.

But they were not to remain long in the "Big Basement": it was still not large enough. A former convent was up for sale: with the help of some generous donations and the hope of fruitful collecting rounds, the House of the Cross was purchased in February 1842. They moved there in the following month of September.

On May 29, 1842, the associates held a meeting, at which the Abbé Le Pailleur was present: they wanted to become more firmly organized, with an eye to the future. They added a few points to their rule of life, adopted as official the name of *Servants of the Poor*, chose Jeanne as their Superior and promised her obedience. In this way, by a development as inconspicuous as that of a bud unfolding, the little society slowly took on the features of a religious community. Jeanne let herself be guided by the events of life, in which she recognized the voice of the Spirit of God.

Begging for the poor
(1842-1852)

"Sister Jeanne, go out instead of us, beg for us." This was what the old women used to say, who during long years had lived by begging. By this they emphasized the very heart of the activity of begging, which was going to become so much a part of Jeanne's life. She was going to substitute herself for the poor, identify herself with them; or rather, guided by the Spirit of Jesus, to recognize that the poor were her "own flesh" (Is. 58:7). Their distress was her distress, their begging was her begging.

Practical considerations led her to do the begging herself: if she had allowed the good women (as she affectionately called them) to go the rounds of the town, as they used to before she had given them shelter, she would have exposed them to many evils, especially those of them who were given to drink. So, she respectfully asked each to give her the addresses of her benefactors and then did the rounds herself instead. She used to explain, "Well, sir, the little old woman won't be coming any more. I shall be coming instead. Please be so kind as to go on giving us your alms." Note the us.

It was not an easy decision to take. Jeanne was proud. To be sure, in her earlier years she had seen the sailors' wives of Cancale coming graciously to each other's help by taking up a collection, but this was not sufficient to make her cheerfully take to begging. In her old age, she still recalled the victory over self which this had frequently required. "I used to go out with my basket, looking for something for our poor … It cost me a lot to do this, but I did it for God and for our dear poor … "

In this she was helped by a Brother of Saint John of God, Claude-Marie

Gandet. The Brothers at that time had a fervent community at Dinan, and a hospital. They were to play an important part in Jeanne's search for the right methods to adopt. It happened one day that Brother Gandet arrived at the "Big Basement," himself collecting for the Brothers' hospital. He found Jeanne extremely perplexed. They understood each other, and he helped her make the deliberate choice of going out to beg. To encourage her, he promised to support her and introduce her to a number of families whom he himself used to visit. It is even said that he presented her with her first begging basket.

So Jeanne became a beggar-maid. She asked for money, but also for gifts in kind: food – the remains of meals or leftovers were often particularly appreciated – things, clothes. "I should be very grateful if you could give me a spoonful of salt or a small piece of butter." "We could do with a cauldron for boiling the sheets." "A little wool or filasse (hemp) would be useful to us … " She was not shy to express her faith: if she happened to be asking for some wood to make a bed, she would be specific and say, "I should like a little wood to relieve a member of Jesus Christ."

She was not always so well received. In the course of one round, she rang a rich and miserly old man's doorbell. Knowing how to get on the right side of him, she persuaded him to give her a good contribution. Next day, she called again. This time, he was angry. She smiled, "But, sir, my poor were hungry yesterday, they are hungry again today, and tomorrow they will be hungry too." He gave again, and promised to go on giving. Thus, with a smile, she knew how to invite the rich to think again and discover their responsibilities.

One incident has become famous. An irritable old bachelor struck her. Gently she replied, "Thank you; that was for me. Now please give me something for my poor!"

She often used to apply for help at the Welfare Office and in the early days she was treated as a member of the organization. But one day a woman employee was rude to her and told her to take her place in the queue with the beggars. She obeyed. She was a beggar after all, it was the right place for her.

Jeanne as the collecting Sister; statue by Angel Acosta.

When things were going badly, she would drum up her courage. She would say to her companion, "Let's go on for God!" Or, one feast day at Saint-Servan, with one of those half-smiles characteristic of her: "Today, we're going to make a good collection. Our old folk have had a good dinner, so St. Joseph ought to be pleased at seeing his dependents being well looked after. He is going to bless us!"

It seems she had a quality of presence which impressed people, and a sort of charm which worked on them. One man, who knew her well, has this delightful formula: "She had a gift for speech, a grace in asking ... She collected by praising God, you might say."

Conducted thus, collecting became transfigured. It might have aroused a simple reaction of giving, by which rich people could salve their consciences; but Jeanne made it a work of evangelization, causing people to search their consciences and encouraging a change of heart.

Thanks to the collecting, the little society's activities could expand. They had no qualms in moving into the House of the Cross, and in the month of November 1842, twenty-six old ladies were living there, some of them quite infirm. All this required a lot of work.

Madeleine Bourges came full time to join the associates. She and Virginie stopped doing their professional work outside; all their time henceforth was to be devoted to the service of the persons they had taken in. A short time afterwards, Marie Jamet did the same. From then on, the begging alone was to assure their livelihood – and finish paying off the house.

A doctor, who had known Jeanne at the hospital of Le Rosais, was overjoyed to see her in charge of the House of the Cross; he consented to treat the old people free of charge, and right up to 1857, he was to show immense devotion to them.

An important event took place during the winter of 1842-43: the admission of the first old man. Jeanne's attention had been drawn to an old sailor, alone and sick in a damp cellar; she found him in a most deplorable state, in rags, on rotten straw, haggard of face. Moved by the liveliest compassion, Jeanne went off, confided to a charitable acquaintance what she had just seen and came back a moment later with a shirt and clean clothes. She washed him, changed his clothes for him and took him back to the house. There he recovered his strength. He was called Rodolphe Laisné. Other men very soon came to join him there.

From time to time, new collaboration or arising needs gave the begging a new boost, or widened its scope. One day, a lady named Mademoiselle Dubois offered to accompany Jeanne to collect with her in the neighboring villages. She was a woman of some social standing, which she compromised by going begging with Jeanne. Her presence caught people's imagination and they gave more freely. As well as money, they were given wheat, buck-wheat, potatoes, and also thread and cloth, and new friendships were built up.

They collected leftovers more assiduously than ever. Now and again they organized a great collection of clothing. They began collecting in markets and, in the port of Saint Malo, at the ships. In buying the House of the Cross, they incurred the heavy debt of twenty thousand francs. Within two and a half years, that is by the end of 1844, with seven years still in hand, Jeanne had paid off the lot.

Sometimes a gift turned up unexpectedly. Thus it was when the nephew of a former fishwife, whose reputation was extremely bad, saw for himself the marvel: received into the House of the Cross, she had become another woman and had recovered her dignity. Astonished, the good man bequeathed seven thousand francs to the home – and died not long afterwards.

This money arrived just in time to pay for the roofing of a new building, which was in construction in spite of their having nothing in reserve: except for one fifty centime coin which they put at the foot of Our Lady's statue. Everyone lent a hand. Some folk gave building stones, others cement, others free cartage, and others hours of work. The Sisters wielded shovel and trowel. And, to pay off the three thousand francs still owing, the Montyon Prize arrived just at the right moment.

This was a prize which the French Academy attributed each year to a French man or woman of the poorer classes who had accomplished the most meritorious action. The friends of the home insisted that Jeanne be nominated for this, and she finally agreed. The Mayor of Saint-Servan and the leading citizens of the town signed an address to the Academy, and on December 11, 1845, before a distinguished audience which included Victor Hugo, Lamartine, Chateaubriand, Theirs and many other celebrities, Monsieur Dupin, Sr., delivered a resounding eulogy on humble Jeanne. The newspapers covered the event. The speech was put into print.

Jeanne realized that she could make use of this speech: wherever she went begging from then on she took with her the "Academy Pamphlet," as she used to call it, and it became a very effective recommendation for her. She made use of it, as well, in her collecting rounds over new territory: Dinan, Rennes, Tours, Angers, and many other towns throughout France.

For ten years, from 1842-1852, Jeanne was to devote herself to the begging, almost without interruption. And never once was she disappointed by the One in Whom she had placed all her confidence. To everyone's astonishment, the number of old people kept increasing; they were happy, and well cared for; the house was enlarged, and they were about to acquire other houses … with nothing in hand, no assured income. No explanation other than Jeanne's tireless begging, the collective effort of a city stimulated by her, and her faith in God's indefectible love for his poor.

Jeanne Jugan is awarded
the Montyon Prize; the French
Academy is in the background.
Detail of icon by George
and Sergio Pinecross.
Photo © Willy Berry.

Painting by Léon Raffin (1982) entitled "Jeanne's Route," depicting Jeanne Jugan
on her begging rounds.

Sisters of the Poor

L ittle by little, Jeanne and her small group of friends had become aware that they were leading a religious life and they took steps towards its organization.

By now they had taken vows – private vows, not yet official vows – of obedience and of chastity. They had already begun to wear something like a uniform style of dress which, in fact, resembled that customarily worn by the local peasant folk. Like the Brothers of Saint John of God, the Sisters were wearing a little crucifix and a leather belt. And finally, they had adopted "religious names": Jeanne would now be called Sister Mary of the Cross.

In December 1843, she was re-elected Superior. But lo and behold, only two weeks later, the Abbé Le Pailleur, by his sole authority, quashed this election and appointed as Superior the timid Marie Jamet, aged twenty-three, who was his penitent. She would be more pliable in his hands than Jeanne Jugan, who was fifty-one years old, well experienced in life and known in Saint-Servan for the last twenty-six years. Besides, she never addressed herself to him for spiritual advice.

The priest had spoken: in that era, what could a group of ordinary women do? They bowed to his decision. But for Jeanne, doubtless it was not without anguish and anxiety.

Life went on. Besides, people outside the little group knew nothing of the change: Jeanne remained, in the opinion of all, the authority behind the work undertaken.

At the beginning of the year 1844, the Association officially changed its name: the Sisters chose to be called Sisters of the Poor, no doubt to better underline that evangelical brotherliness willed by Jesus, and their intention of sharing completely, on an equal footing, with those brothers and sisters.

After that, the Sisters took for one year private vows of poverty and of hospitality: this fourth vow – by which they consecrated themselves to receiving the elderly poor – drew its inspiration from a long established custom of the Brothers of Saint John of God.

In January 1844, Eulalie Jamet had followed her elder sister Marie to the House of the Cross. Towards the close of 1845, a new Sister joined the little group: Françoise Trévily became the sixth Sister of the Poor.

And in the following year, a decisive step forward would be taken: the foundation of a second house.

In the month of January 1846, Jeanne set out for Rennes. She was going there to beg for the needs of the poor at Saint-Servan. She got the local newspapers to announce her arrival: it was only the month before, in fact, that they had been writing about her, telling of the Montyon Prize and giving the text of Monsieur Dupin's speech to the French Academy.

Right from the start, it was the beggars who caught Jeanne's eye: less numerous, in proportion, than those at Saint-Servan, but many were elderly and in great need of assistance. And there was much misery in the poorer sections of the town. It was not long before a project for a foundation began to form in Jeanne's mind, and she asked her Superior's approval.

And then she set to work. She met influential people, sometimes not very well disposed. Undaunted, she gently insisted: "Quite so, an act of madness, you might say an impossibility … But if God is with us, it will come about!" And how could it be otherwise when it was a question of her poor?

Marie Jamet came to Rennes to join Jeanne. By this time, Jeanne

A room in the original home in Rennes, preserved much as Jeanne Jugan would have known it.

had already rented a large room with a smaller room attached to it. Before long, there were ten old ladies.

A bigger house had to be found. The two Sisters went in search of one, but in vain. They confided the affair to Saint Joseph (who was to take an increasingly important part in the prayers of the Little Sisters of the Poor). On March 19, his feast day, Marie was praying in the church of All Saints. Someone came up to her and said, "Have you got a house?" "Not yet." "I've just the thing for you." Off they went to see it. The house, lying in the suburbs of La Madeleine could accommodate forty or fifty poor people, and a dependent building would serve as chapel. With the agreement of Saint-Servan, the contract was signed on March 25, and they moved in the same day. Some soldiers helped with the transport of the old ladies and the moving in. The household continued to expand, in poverty.

Happily, some young girls of Saint-Servan had entered as postulants. Soon, some from Rennes came to join them, then from other districts.

Jeanne had resumed her begging rounds: Vitré Fougeres … And wherever she went, her very presence seemed like an appeal. It frequently came about that, after her visit, young women would apply to enter the novitiate.

It was perhaps about now that Jeanne got as far as Redon. She rang the doorbell of the Eudist college (she was somewhat of a Eudist herself). One of the priests related, "I went to see her in the parlor and she electrified me. Without more ado, I took her into our senior boarders' study-room. There were about a hundred of them in it … and Jeanne in simple and direct terms explained the object of her mission. Amazed and deeply moved, all those pupils emptied out everything in their pockets and desks."

For some years already, the Sisters had benefited from the advice of Father Félix Massot, a former Provincial of the Hospitaller Brothers of Saint John of God. In the spring of 1846, they elaborated a rule which embraced more than the few original statutes. Very many points of this text drew their inspiration directly from the constitutions of the Brothers. But the spiritual influence deriving from Saint John Eudes remained clearly present, especially in several aspects of their daily prayer life.

Some time later on, as a result of one of Jeanne's collecting rounds, a third house was opened at Dinan, in one of the old bastions of the city wall. As soon as possible though, they moved away to somewhere less dismal, thence to a former convent. We shall have more to recount about this old bastion in the following chapter.

Jeanne begged without respite. In January 1847, we find her at Saint-Brieuc. A local newspaper presented her thus: "Jeanne Jugan, the woman so devoted to the service of the unfortunate, who has worked miracles

The room in the first home in Dinan where Father Félix Massot helped Jeanne draft the first rule of life of the growing community.

of charity and about whom the Breton press had so much to say last year, is now within our walls. She is making a collection for her work. Visiting charitable people, she merely says, 'I am Jeanne Jugan.' The name alone is enough to open all purses."

And all the time Jeanne kept on walking, "her bag slung across her shoulder and her basket over her arm," begging on behalf of the aged poor, or sometimes to help one of the recently founded houses: Saint-Servan, Rennes, Dinan, and then Tours (1849).

For even though the control of the work was no longer in her hands, she had to save it from disaster on several occasions, since she was the one whom people were prepared to trust and since she was the one who could see what needed to be done. She would arrive, take the necessary decisions, obtain the funds that were lacking, encourage this person or that, then disappear; she was needed elsewhere. She had "nowhere to rest her head"; she did not seem to belong to any particular local community. Provided that the poor old people were housed, cared for, loved, she consented to be without hearth and home for herself.

7

An English tourist and a French journalist write about Jeanne

L et us go back a bit. At the beginning of August 1846, Jeanne and Marie Jamet had taken possession of an ancient bastion, in the city walls of Dinan.

Three weeks later, an English tourist knocked at the door: he had come to see Jeanne Jugan.

He later published an article describing his visit, of which the following is a partial reproduction:

"To reach the floor where they were living, you had to negotiate an awkward spiral stair; the ceiling of the room was low, the walls were bare and rough, the windows narrow and grilled, so that you might have imagined you were in a cavern or a prison; but this dismal look was to some extent enlivened by the firelight and the happy appearance of the people inside …

"Jeanne received us kindly … she was simply but cleanly dressed in a black dress and white cap and kerchief; this is the dress adopted by the community. She looks about fifty years old, is of medium height with a sunburnt complexion, she looks worn out though her expression is serene and full of kindness; there is not the slightest trace of pretentiousness or conceit detectable in it."

A veritable interview then took place between the tourist – himself a person of standing, at the time busily preparing to found a hospice for the aged – and our Jeanne Jugan. She gave straightforward answers to his questions.

"She never knew on any given day, she said, where the next day's provisions would come from, but she persevered, in the firm conviction that God would never abandon the poor, and acted according to this certain principle: that everything we do for them, we do for Our Lord Jesus Christ.

"I asked her how she could tell which were the ones truly deserving to be helped; she replied that she admitted those who applied to her and seemed to be the most destitute; that she began with the aged and infirm as being those most in need; and that she used to make enquiries from their neighbors as to their character, means, etc.

"Rather than leave those idle who could still set their hand to something useful, she made them unravel and card old bits of material, and then spin the wool thus recovered; by such means they are able to earn six liards a day. They also did other work as occasion would allow and received a third of the small return obtained."

Jeanne then described what she might expect from various tradespeople: foodstuffs still fit to eat but not so easy to sell.

"I told her that having covered France, she ought to come to England and teach us how to care for our own poor people. She replied that, with God's help, she would do so if invited.

"There is something so calm, so holy about this woman that, seeing her, I felt as though I were in the presence of a higher being, and her words went so much to my heart that my eyes – I know not why – filled with tears.

"That is Jeanne Jugan, the friend of the Brittany poor, and the sight of her alone would be enough to compensate for the horrors of a day and a night spent on the stormy sea."

Some two years later, an article on Jeanne and her work was published by the Paris newspaper "*L'Univers*," whose editor-in-chief was none other than Louis Veuillot. This great Catholic journalist had had occasion to visit the recently founded house at Tours. A short time afterwards, he was present at the National Assembly, during a debate

Portrait of Jeanne Jugan by Léon Brune, completed in 1855 during one of her collecting rounds. Jeanne often stayed at the château of the family de la Grasserie, who commissioned Brune to do the portrait without Jeanne's knowledge.

on the *right to assistance* written into the preamble to the new Constitution of 1848 – which was not to his liking.

On leaving the chamber, he wrote a resounding article to introduce the parliamentarians, so he said, to "someone more versed in socialism than the lot of you." He meant Jeanne Jugan.

"She loved the poor because she loved God. One day she begged her confessor to teach her how to love God even more. 'Jeanne,' he said, 'up to now you have been giving to the poor; from now on, you must share with them.' … That same evening, Jeanne had a companion."

The article goes on to relate Veuillot's visit to the house at Tours: "I saw clean clothes, happy faces, and even radiant health. Between the youthful Sisters and these old people reigns a mutual affection and respect to gladden the heart …

"The nuns conform in every respect to the regime of their poor people, and there is no difference whatever, except that the Sisters serve and the poor are served … Everything happens pat for the needs of the moment. At supper, nothing is left over; at dinner, nothing is lacking. Charity provided the house. When a new resident turns up, charity provides a bed and clothes" (*L'Univers*, September 13, 1848).

L'Univers had quite a large circulation, and this article of Veuillot helped to make the work of the Sisters of the Poor more widely known.

Growth

From the very first, the mother-house and the novitiate had been located at the former Convent of the Cross, at Saint-Servan. But by the end of 1847, there was no longer sufficient place there to accommodate the fifteen or so postulants and novices who had begun their formation, as well as the elderly poor.

Since Abbé Le Pailleur, Marie Jamet's counselor, had had a few misunderstandings with the Bishop of Rennes, they decided to make the transfer to the recently founded house at Tours.

From that time on, the number of young girls was constantly on the increase: by the summer of 1849, there were already forty.

However, some months beforehand, Jeanne's Sisters had summoned her to Tours, to that house she had not herself founded. She arrived there in February 1849. The principal matter in hand was to obtain official authorizations, which had not been granted.

She was welcomed with enthusiasm by Monsieur Dupont, a generous and saintly layman, who had spent much of his time and money to prepare the way for the Sisters: "For the last two days we have been honored to have with us Jeanne Jugan, the mother of all the Little Sisters … What admirable trust in God! What love for His Holy Name! She will do much good for us at Tours. Benighted worldlings suppose that this poor beggar-maid, as she calls herself, will ask them for alms; but if their eyes were opened, they too would understand that they receive a greater alms from her by hearing her speak so lovingly and simply about God's Providence."

One letter written at this period has been preserved: young Sister Pauline wrote from Tours to Abbé Le Pailleur (February 19, 1849). She told him about the visits she had paid to their benefactors and to the Bishop, accompanied by Sister Jeanne. Then they had been to see the parish priest, who had advised them to go back and see the Bishop again and ask him for a letter of recommendation to the clergy. They had gone to him. In reading the continuation of this letter we get a vivid glimpse of Jeanne, and of her behavior in the Congregation, ten years after its first beginnings. "The Bishop told her that he did not dare to move too fast. She went down on her knees, she left him entirely free to decide as his great charity might dictate. He was touched by this and told her to wait a few days and he would do it ... We only wish that Monsieur d'Outremont" (a friend of the house and a member of the Saint Vincent de Paul Society) "were in Tours, to get him to put a word or two in the paper about Sister Jeanne. She tells me that this would be very useful, and that she has been into several shops and found people as hard-hearted as brooms ...

"We have been to see the Prefect's wife, who received us kindly and the same evening sent us a permit for the whole Department from her husband, whom we had not been able to see ...

"I am very happy to have Sister Jeanne, she is very kind, she likes it here at Tours but is a little upset at the thought of still not being able to go collecting ...

"I think Sister Catherine will be suitable to go collecting. Sister Jeanne likes her very much." Finally, Jeanne left the house at Tours on a solid footing, and well rooted in the hearts of the people there.

On August 1, a new foundation began: a house in Paris. This had been requested by the members of the Saint Vincent de Paul Society, who had come to know of the work through Monsieur d'Outremont. And towards the end of that same year 1849, two other houses came into being, one a Besançon and the other at Nantes. It was at Nantes that the name "*Little Sisters of the Poor*" became current, to be adopted as the official name a little later on. Popular intuition had hit on the epithet expressing Jeanne Jugan's intention: excluding all domination, to become little, so as to love more.

Jeanne had played no direct part in the foundations at Paris, Besançon or Nantes. But it was she, on the other hand, who brought that of Angers into existence. Here is how it came about.

Untiringly engaged in her collecting rounds, Jeanne arrived in Angers in December 1849, where a number of families were eagerly awaiting her. She had come with the intention of begging alms for the foundations already made, but from the outset she had in mind (as in Rennes) to endow the city of Angers, where she had been given such a warm welcome, with an establishment for the elderly poor.

Thanks to a priest, a Vicar General at Rennes, a house was readily made available and the foundation was made in April 1850. In the meantime, Jeanne had presumably gone back to Tours with the proceeds of her collecting, and had set off to collect in other towns. And so, on April 3 she returned to Angers, accompanied by Marie Jamet and two young Sisters. Monseigneur Angebault, the Bishop, received them with open arms. As elsewhere, they arrived empty-handed: the four of them had only six francs between them to open the establishment.

They received the necessary permits for the collecting, moved into their premises, and set about soliciting alms. Two days later, Marie left again for Tours, "already consoled." Two postulants from Angers went with her. At the end of the month, the first old people were admitted.

Gifts in kind were particularly abundant and yet, one day, they were short of butter, and Jeanne saw the old people eating dry bread. "But this is the land of butter!" she exclaimed. " Why on earth don't you ask Saint Joseph for some?" She lit a night-light in front of a status of Jesus' foster-father, had all the empty butter dishes fetched, and propped up a card: "Good Saint Joseph, send us butter for our old folk!" Visitors were amazed or amused at such simplicity of heart: very reasonably, one of them expressed his doubts about the efficacy of whole procedure. But, hidden underneath these simple gestures: what tremendous faith! A few days later, an anonymous donor sent a very large amount of butter, and all the dishes were filled.

Following the visit of the mysterious English tourist, plans were set in motion for a foundation in England. The first house was opened in London in 1851. This painting by James Collinson depicts life in one of the early English homes of the Little Sisters.

Jeanne wanted the poor folks home to be cheerful. On the strength of her friendly contacts in Anjou, she went one day to see the colonel commanding one of the units of the Angers garrison and asked him to send some of the regimental bondsmen to make her old folk happy. "I'll send you the whole band!" The Angers brass-band provided a merry accompaniment to that self-giving love arousing love in others.

From Angers, Jeanne journeyed to other towns, to other fields of collecting. During the winter of 1850-1851, we catch glimpses of her at Dinan, at Lorient and at Brest.

In this latter town, she met a lady active in good works, but who did not give her much encouragement. Jeanne listened to what she had to say, thought for a while, then decided: "'Very well, dear lady, we'll try!"

Accompanied by a friend, she set about collecting. They came to one house where her friend expected a cold reception, and suggested they pass it by. But Jeanne, grabbing the bell-rope, replied, "We'll ring in God's name, and God will bless us." The donation was generous.

While she was thus engaged in awakening folk to their duty of sharing, and in collecting their gifts, Jeanne kept her eye on the family that she brought into existence. Following that of Angers, foundations were begun in Bordeaux, Rouen and Nancy. Jeanne was not directly involved in any of these however.

Then came the first house in England, in the suburbs of London. We must add here that, some time earlier, Charles Dickens had been in Paris, and had paid a visit to the Sisters' newly founded home. Deeply impressed, he wrote about this visit in his weekly *Household Words* (February 14, 1852). Beginning with a brief account of how the work began, he went on to describe the house in the Rue Saint Jacques: "One old fellow has his feet upon a little foot-warmer, and thinly pipes out that he is very comfortable now, for he is always warm. The chills of age and the chills of the cold pavement remain together in his memory – but he is very comfortable now, very comfortable." This article of the famous novelist was of great assistance to the Little Sisters of the Poor in establishing themselves in his homeland.

Keeping pace with the geographical and numerical growth (in 1853 there would be five hundred Sisters), the Institute itself was in the process of development: the rule was being completed and taking final shape. Father Félix Massot and the Abbé Le Pailleur worked together on it in 1851 for three weeks at Lille. This draft was submitted to the bishop of Rennes and, on the May 29, 1852, Monseigneur Brossais Saint-Marc signed the decree approving the statutes: from then on, the family of the Little Sisters of the Poor was to be a proper religious Congregation within the Church.

This episcopal approval made Abbé Le Pailleur officially the Father Superior General of the Congregation, in conjunction with Marie Jamet, the Mother General. Things had turned out just as he had hoped, and he was satisfied.

He took up residence in the house at Rennes. As a matter of fact, a spacious property on the outskirts of Rennes, called La Piletière, had just been purchased, sufficient to accommodate not only the personnel of the Rennes foundation, but also the novitiate and the mother-house. These latter, having in the meantime been transferred from Tours to Paris, now moved in as well. And on May 31 the bishop came to visit them and to preside over the Clothing of twenty-four postulants and the Profession of seventeen novices.

9

"You have stolen my work from me."

ᥞ(1852-1856)ᥨ

The strange behavior of the Abbé Le Pailleur – can only be explained by a subtle but doubtless deep defect in his psychological make-up.

Already in 1843 he had quashed Jeanne's re-election as Superior, in order to confide this responsibility to Marie Jamet, his spiritual daughter. As the years went on, his hold over the work grew gradually stronger, while all the time it was Jeanne who, tirelessly, was collecting for the new houses, working directly at two foundations, hurrying hither and thither to prop up or rescue those which were on the verge of collapse, assuring by her presence or her reputation, the worth and the vitality of the initiatives undertaken for the relief of destitute old people.

Blessed with episcopal approval and henceforth installed in the mother-house, Abbé Le Pailleur made a decision which was to completely change Jeanne's existence: he summoned her to the mother-house. From that day onwards, Jeanne would no longer sustain her contacts with benefactors, nor would she have any occupation worthy of note within her Congregation: she was to live out her life hidden behind the walls of La Piletière, engaged in humdrum tasks.

Jeanne was barely sixty years old, and in full activity. She obeyed humbly. Devoid of all responsibility, she was to remain at the mother-house first at Rennes, then at La Tour Saint Joseph near the village of Saint-Pern until her death twenty-seven years later.

At La Piletière she was to live buried in littleness, known only as Sister Mary of the Cross. Within the Congregation, the name Jeanne Jugan was scarcely ever used again; but for so many people in the world outside, how lively the memory of it remained!

For the first few years her task was to direct the manual work of the postulants, of whom there were very many: sixty-four, in fact, in 1853. The kindness and gentleness with which she treated her young sisters is on record; she had always loved the young and won their love in return.

She lived in complete self-effacement, never once asserting her rights. Many years later, one Sister was to write of her: "I never heard her utter the slightest word which might have led us to imagine that she had been the first Superior General. She used to speak with great respect and deference of our first *Good Mothers* (i.e. Superiors). She was so little, so respectful in her relations with them … "

She saw one of her first Sisters, Virginie Trédaniel, die at the age of thirty-two. Was it this death, or her own sufferings, or the memory of the trying times of the first foundation? One day she said to the postulants: "We have been grafted on to the Cross."

This graft was healthy and strong, and the Church acknowledged it as her own. On July 9, 1854, His Holiness Pope Pius IX approved the Congregation of the Little Sisters of the Poor. What a profound joy for Jeanne's faith.

In order to pass himself off as founder and Superior General of this new Institute, the Abbé Le Pailleur had managed, little by little, to distort the history of its origins. For the next thirty-six years the young girls who entered the Congregation were taught a purely fictitious account, where Jeanne was presented only as the third Little Sister.

As for the Abbé himself, the marks of respect that he expected to be shown became more and more exaggerated. He wielded an absolute authority over the Congregation. Everything had to pass through his hands. He it was who made every decision, who had to be consulted for everything.

But the astonishment, nay the scandal, that all this provoked

Hidden away at the motherhouse: In 1852 Jeanne began her long retirement among the novices and postulants at the house in Rennes. She would move to the permanent motherhouse, near St. Pern, in 1856.

eventually came to the notice of those in high places. The Holy See decided to open an inquiry into the matter, and in 1890 Abbé Le Pailleur was removed from office and summoned to Rome; there, he ended his days in a monastery.

For more than forty years, Marie Jamet had remained docile and submissive to him. She thought she was doing the right thing, but she had often been torn between what she considered to be her duty of obedience and her respect for the truth. A short time before her death, she said openly: "I am not the first Little Sister, nor the foundress of the work. Jeanne Jugan was the first one and the foundress of the Little Sisters of the Poor."

As for Jeanne, both sorrow and confidence were mingled in her heart as the years passed by. She was clearsighted, and could not approve of what was going on, but her faith rose above all this scheming. She retained sufficient liberty of heart to smilingly tell the Abbé Le Pailleur one day what she thought of him: "You have stolen my work from me ... but I willingly give it to you!"

No regular income!

❧(1856-1865)❧

In the spring of 1856, Jeanne was to change her abode: she accompanied the group of novices and postulants who were moving to La Tour Saint Joseph, a vast property in the village of Saint-Pern, thirty-five kilometers from Rennes. This newly acquired property would now house both the novitiate and the mother-house.

Here, Jeanne continued her life as before: quite hidden from the public eye and occupied with lowly tasks. For several years, together with two novices, she slept in a little dormitory called "the bell room."

She was carefully excluded from all responsibility, given no marks of honor. Nominally, she was a member of the General Council of the Congregation, but was never called upon to attend.

But yes once, once only, was she invited to share in its deliberations. She did so. Her signature attests it. It was June 19, 1885.

A grave problem had arisen which would affect the life of the Institute. It was a matter which called into question the very essential of the vocation of the Little Sisters: the exigencies of poverty within the Congregation.

From the very beginning they had wanted to live poorly with the poor and, together with them, depend solely on charity. And so, any fixed source of income had been excluded. Ownership was limited to the buildings they occupied, and which assured them independence and security.

In actual fact, there was no written regulation supporting this choice. And it had come about, in the first years, that the Congregation had accepted

Section of the novitiate at La Tour St. Joseph where Jeanne lived for many years, as it appears today. Her room was situated directly below the clock; today it is a place of prayer and pilgrimage.

a few small investments or endowments. But these had remained the exception.

Now, in 1865, legacy of 4,000 francs bequeathed in the form of regular income, had been left to the Congregation. Once again, the question arose: were they to accept it? While the Council hesitated, a friend of the Sisters, who was helping them to administer their finances, reminded them of the principle at stake: "If you will allow me to give my humble opinion, you should accept it only if authorized to forego the interest and to use the capital sum to pay for your house (in Paris). You should own only the houses you live in, and otherwise to live on daily charity. If the Little Sisters were thought to have investments, they would lose their right to that charity which kept the Israelites alive in the wilderness, and if once they were to start storing up manna, the manna would go bad in their hands, as happened long ago to God's people."

This was daring advice: it was the period of the upsurge of capitalism; the great French banks were being set up and developing; check books had just been invented; and the Comtesse de Ségur herself wrote "La Fortune de Gaspar"! All that people could talk about was how to make a profit, and the pursuit of money had become a sort of religion.

But the Little Sisters of the Poor, responsive to the warning they had received, were about to choose to possess nothing.

The sewing room of the novitiate of La Tour Saint Joseph. It was here that Jeanne spent more than 20 years, humbly mingling with the novices.

First of all they asked several bishops for their opinion; then the General Council met. It was to this meeting that Sister Mary of the Cross was summoned. She seems to have been surprised, even startled: "I am only a poor ignorant woman; what can I contribute?" But they insisted. "Since you wish it, I shall obey."

So she came to the meeting. She expressed her opinion clearly: the right thing to do was to go on refusing any regular income and rely on charity.

This was the viewpoint that was adopted. The circular which was sent to all the houses stated precisely: "The Congregation cannot own investments or any regular income of a permanent sort," and that consequently "we shall refuse any legacy or gift consisting of investments or entailing the endowment of beds or Masses or any other kind of permanent obligation."

Thereupon, the Council wrote to the Imperial Minister of Justice and Religious Affairs, informing him of this decision. The government gave its official agreement the following year, taking note, by virtue of the same, of the refusal of this legacy of 4,000 francs.

A little later, we find Jeanne encouraging the young Sisters to pray "that there be no giving in to the entreaties of those who wanted to give us stocks and shares."

This shows us how she was keeping prayerful watch over this Congregation she had brought into existence, and over that free choice of poverty which surrendered it to the loving care of God, their Heavenly Father.

The simple wisdom of Sister Mary of the Cross

❦(1865-1879)❧

The years passed by. No outstanding events occurred at La Tour Saint Joseph.

Nothing, that is, except a lone figure catching our attention from time to time ... with her rosary in her hands: Sister Mary of the Cross, "upright, supporting herself with a big walking-stick ... walked the fields and woods of La Tour Saint Joseph, giving thanks to God ... and whenever she saw old friends who knew something of the beginnings of the work ... she would sing her Magnificat. (She) was truly eloquent in her simplicity."

And as well, scattered here and there along the years, words of simple wisdom – often picturesque, sometimes comic. For example, one day she told the novices how they should act if disagreeable things were said to them: "You have to be like a sack of wool, closing over the stone without a sound." And again: "You must do penance." What does that mean? She sketches a concrete example. "Two Little Sisters are out collecting; they have a lot to carry; it is raining, windy, they are wet, etc. If they accept these discomforts bravely, submitting to the Will of God, they are doing penance!" One day she called a young Sister over to an open window; she showed her some stonemasons. "Look at those workmen cutting the white stone for the chapel, and how fine they make the stone look. You must let Our Lord form you like that!"

Sister Claire was running at top speed along a corridor. Jeanne stopped her: "You're leaving someone behind you." The Sister turned around, intrigued. "Excuse me, my good Little Sister, but I can't see anyone." "Yes, you are! You're leaving God behind! He is letting you run on ahead, for Our Lord never used to go so fast, and was never in a hurry like you are!"

The recollections of those years which have come down to our day give us a host of delightful sayings. There are also a few recollections which are more striking. For example, one day the mother of a family went into the chapel with her children. One little fellow, although already four or five years old, could not walk. She still had to carry him. As often before, she came to pray, asking for him to be cured. She came out, still carrying the child in her arms. She met Jeanne. The latter took him for his mother, then put him down on the ground, saying: "Little one, what a weight you are!" She let him hold her walking stick and, lo and behold, he began walking of his own accord. "Little John's walking," exclaimed his mother. "He's walking with Jeanne Jugan's stick."

And so the years went by. About 1870, Jeanne moved from the bell room to the infirmary room, which she shared with three other Sisters until her death.

She kept abreast of events: the distressing incidents of the war of 1870; the First Vatican Council, too quickly interrupted; the fall of Rome to the revolutionaries struggling for the unification of Italy. She took great interest also in the apostolic work of the Congregation, and the priests attached to the house gladly came to see her when they returned from their travels, telling her all they had done and asking for her prayers. The one among them who contributed most to the expansion of the Congregation outside France – Father Ernest Lelièvre, a native of the North – particularly loved to recommend himself to her prayers.[1]

---

[1] The Congregation owes its rapid expansion, especially in Great Britain, Ireland, the United States, Italy, Malta and Spain to Father Lelièvre. "Have the poor ever had a greater friend than he?" asked Msgr. Baunard in the 502-page biography he dedicated to him in 1923. This book, now out of print, has been condensed into a booklet published for the centenary of his death: *Ernest Lelièvre*, 1826-1889. The English edition is available from the publications office of the Little Sisters of the Poor in Baltimore, Maryland.

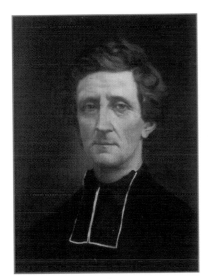

Father Ernest Lelièvre, who was responsible for the rapid expansion of the Congregation.

She rejoiced in the beauty of the surroundings, the flowers on the grounds. One day, she showed one to a young Sister. "Do you know who made that?" "God did," replied the Sister. Jeanne looked her in the eye, and said in admiration, "Our Bridegroom did!"

Prayer became more and more the center of her daily life. Her devotion to the Eucharist, to Our Lord's Passion (including the Way of the Cross), her love for our Blessed Lady: none of these escaped the novices' eye. Several of these were particularly struck by her radiantly joyful bearing and loving concentration when she made the sign of the cross or approached the Sacrament of Holy Communion. To see her "made one long to love the Eucharist as she loved it." Others were struck by her remarkably tender love for Mary. "It was a pleasure to see her praying with her rosary. She loved to say, 'By the Ave Maria, we shall get to Paradise.'"

"She lived in the presence of God, and was always talking to us about Him," a novice of the time once said. Conversations about prayer were a delight to her. She had invented some quaint sayings to highlight the pathways of the spiritual life: "You must be very little before God. When you pray, begin like this. Imagine yourself a little frog before God." Or again, in moments of crisis, (and this no doubt is a guarded reference to her own behavior): "Go and find Him when your patience and strength give out and your feel alone and helpless. Jesus is waiting for you in the chapel. Say to Him, 'Jesus, you know exactly what is going on. You are all I have, and You know all. Come to my help.' And then go, and don't worry about how you are going to manage. That you have told God about it is enough. He has a good memory."

As for the way of praying, she recommended the path of discretion, especially concerning vocal prayers. Whenever she prayed with the novices "she often used to insist that, later on, we should be careful not to say too many of these prayers of devotion: 'You will weary your old folk,' she used to say. 'They will get bored and go off for a smoke ... even during the rosary!'"

She was always reverting to the aged, and sharing with the young her experiences in their service. "Little ones, you must always be cheerful Our little old folk do not like long faces."

When she spoke of the poor, "her heart used to overflow ... 'Dear children,' she would say, 'let us love God dearly, and the poor in him.' 'With the eye of faith, we must see Jesus in our old people – for they are God's mouthpiece.'"

She used to give the Sisters pieces of advice which, while simple, were charged with meaning; "You mustn't begrudge your efforts in cooking for them anymore than in looking after them when they are ill. Be like a mother to the grateful ones, and also to those who don't know how to be grateful for everything you do for them. Say in your heart, 'I do it for You, my Jesus!' Look on the Poor with compassion, and Jesus will look kindly on you on your last day."

She often used to make reference to the begging: "Do not be afraid of devoting yourself to, and begging for, the poor as I have done, for they are the suffering members of Our Lord."

She had always reflected before acting, and knew what a precious habit it was: "Little ones, you must pray and think before you act. I myself have done this all my life. I used to weigh my every word." She, who so seldom spoke about herself, here confides to us one of her secrets.

Another secret: the love of littleness. "Be little, little, little; if you get big and proud, the Congregation will fall." "Only the little are pleasing to God."

At eighty years of age, she retained a dignified carriage. A young English woman described her thus: " ... walking with so firm a step, leaning upon the arm of a young Sister with one hand

and upon a stout walking stick with the other, so erect and so alert … in the wide alleys of the garden. That which struck us most about her, was the exceeding sweetness of her smile … "

Sometimes, when with the novices, she would smilingly give a little commentary on some spiritual reading they had just heard. One day there had been something about holy tears. She told the reader to shut the book and said to the Sisters, "Some of you may find this hard to understand and say, 'I can't weep … And I wouldn't want to be weeping all the time!' Don't you worry about holy tears. There's no need to get your eyes wet shedding any! But willingly making a sacrifice, peaceably accepting a rebuke – this counts as holy tears. I'm sure you've wept

Statue of Our Lady in the novitiate garden, where Jeanne often walked with the novices.

like this several times today already … " Wisdom, sound equilibrium, benevolence: Jeanne possessed them all.

Little by little, her sight became weaker, and for the last few years of her life she was almost blind. She used to say, "When you are old, you won't be able to see anymore. Now all I can see is God." Or again, "God sees me; that's enough!"

Not that this prevented her from being joyful, or from telling comic stories and recalling amusing anecdotes. For instance, the story about a rabbit which jumped out of her collecting basket one day, and about the little boys who raced after it and caught it; she gave them two sous each for their trouble!

One Easter Day, she joined a group of Sisters who were at a singing practice. "Come on, little ones, let's sing the glory of our Risen Jesus!" And forthwith, she began to beat time with both arms, singing Alleluia with such ardor that she looked as though she wanted to "leave her old body and follow her Jesus!"

What spirit, what youthfulness! She was pervaded by a continual atmosphere of thanksgiving: "In all things, everywhere, in all circumstances, I repeat: 'Blessed be God.'"

Right up to the end, she loved to sing; especially folk songs, or a sort of round, which she had possibly made up herself:

"The Poor Man is calling us
Aloud and from his heart –
Oh, what Glad Tidings!
Now gladly we'll set out."

Or:

"Never refuse anything,
Do not pick and choose.
For us little beggar-maids
All things have their use."

Or again:

"Jesus blest,
King of the Elect,
Who will be the one to love you best?"

It would seem that the profound and simple union with God in which she lived, and which developed with the increasing deprivations of old age, had made her utterly free and vibrantly joyous.

12

From death to life
(1879)

During the latter years of her life, Jeanne quite often used to speak of her death, and always with complete serenity. One day, she said to a young Sister who had dropped in for a chat, "Sing me the refrain: '*Oh why on this alien shore, must I prolong my stay.*'"

Now and again she would say, "How I long to die … " "You mustn't die," would be the reply. "Yes, yes, I want to; I want to go and see God." But before that day came, an event occurred to make her joy complete.

In November 1878, the first steps had been undertaken towards obtaining the Pope's approbation of the constitutions (the approbation of 1854 had only been ad experimentum). On March 1, 1879, Leo XIII granted the desired confirmation.

At that moment, forty years after the humble beginnings at Saint-Servan, there were 2,400 Little Sisters. Jeanne had completed her work and her long mission of prayer. She could depart.

One August morning of 1879, she seemed to grow weaker. She was given the Sacrament of the Sick. She murmured in prayer: "O Mary, you know you are my mother, do not forsake me! ... Eternal Father, open your gates today to the most wretched of your little daughters, to one though who most earnestly longs to see you!" … and in a fainter voice, "O Mary, my dear mother, come to me. You know I love you and how I long to see you!" Then she quietly passed away.

All those who saw her testified to the boundless peace on her features. She had made her last act of abandonment, with and among the poor, into the loving embrace of our Father.

Room where Jeanne Jugan died on August 29, 1879.

The tomb of Saint Jeanne Jugan in the chapel crypt as it appears today.

13

Her mission continues

"People talk to you about me, but let the matter drop. God knows all." Such was the final piece of advice Jeanne gave to a young Sister, only three days professed, who left La Tour Saint Joseph on March 19, 1876, for Saint-Servan.

To remain in the shadows, to be forgotten: Jeanne had no other ambition. And at the time of her death, this ambition appeared to be achieved.

And yet … ! In 1894, she who had been called upon to guide the Congregation after the death of Marie Jamet, undertook to have its history written. This first work of historical research was published in 1902. Preceding it by three years, was the appearance of a brief obituary notice concerning Jeanne Jugan: it acknowledged her to be "the first Little Sister and the foundress."

With this restitution of "her work," Jeanne's posthumous mission began: it has grown and expanded with the passing of the years. In 1935, the numerous testimonies of those who had known her showed that the time had come to open the diocesan Informatory Process concerning her reputation for sanctity. The following year, Jeanne's mortal remains were transferred from the community cemetery to the chapel crypt. The Second World War brought proceedings to a halt: it was not until July 1970 that the Cause was introduced at Rome. All eyewitnesses having by then disappeared, the Apostolic Process had to issue a judgment on the heroicity of Jeanne's virtues by means of a work of historical research. This documentation was completed in February 1979. It was presented to John Paul II, and the decree of her heroic virtues was promulgated on July 13, just six weeks before the centenary of Jeanne Jugan's death.

Three years later, the medically inexplicable character of a cure was recognized: Antoine Schlatter, an aged Resident of the Home of the Little Sisters of the Poor in Toulon (France), suffering from an advanced stage of Raynaud's disease and threatened with the amputation of one of his hands was instantaneously cured during the course of a novena of prayer imploring Jeanne Jugan's intercession.

By proclaiming her "Blessed" on October 3, 1982, and then canonizing her on October 11, 2009, the Church has proposed Jeanne Jugan as an example for our times.

What then, is her message? Is it still relevant, more than one hundred years after her death?

A forerunner in the field of social and apostolic activity, Jeanne already had, one hundred and fifty years ago, that human and evangelical understanding of "old age" which is not confined to her particular era.

By her hospitaller work in the service of the aged poor, established today in thirty countries, she invites us to a consideration, in the light of faith, of the place and the role of the elderly in our modern societies, their insertion into the family and into the Church, the unique contribution this age has to offer, its riches and its difficulties.[1] She urges us to have that essential attitude of esteem, of mutual comprehension, of friendly exchange, of sharing and of reciprocal aid which must bind the generations together.

But Jeanne's message goes further than that. Someone who knew her very well has said that her special characteristic was "the praise of God." When exposed to contradictions, when humiliated, or confronted

[1] Cf. John Paul II – to the participants of the International Forum on "Active Aging," Castelgandolfo, September 5, 1980.
        – to the aged in Munich, November 19, 1980.
        – to the aged of Australia, a talk given at the Home of the Little Sisters of the Poor in Perth-Glendalough, November 30, 1986. The text of this talk is available in booklet form from the publications office of the Little Sisters of the Poor, Baltimore, Maryland

with adversities, "she pressed forward, always praising God."

This praise was solidly rooted in her faith. Poor together with the poor, and glad to be so, Jeanne possessed absolute confidence in the fatherly goodness of God, abandoned herself to the guidance of His Providence, recognized herself as a useless servant, and proclaimed her joy to "await all from the Good God."

Jeanne Jugan challenges us to live the Beatitudes today. Her mission continues, a mission authenticated by Pope John Paul II in the presence of thousands of pilgrims who came to Rome to celebrate her beatification.

"A close reading of the Positio on the virtues of Jeanne Jugan, as well as of the recent biographies about her and her epic of evangelical charity, inclines me to say that God could glorify no more humble a servant than she," emphasized John Paul II in the homily of the Mass of October 3, 1982. "Jeanne invites all of us," he continued, "and I quote here from the Rule of the Little Sisters, 'to share personally in the beatitude of spiritual poverty, leading to that complete dispossession which commits a soul to God.' She invites us to this much more by her life than by those few words of hers which have been recorded and which are so marked with the seal of the Holy Spirit …

"In her long retirement at La Tour Saint Joseph, many novices and Little Sisters came under her decisive influence and she left on her Congregation the stamp of her spirit by the quiet but eloquent radiance of her life. In our day, pride, the pursuit of efficacy, the temptation to use power all run rampant in the world, and sometimes, unfortunately, even in the Church. They become an obstacle to the coming of the Kingdom of God. This is why the spirituality of Jeanne Jugan can attract the followers of Christ and fill their hearts with simplicity and humility, with hope and evangelical joy, having their source in God and in self-forgetfulness."

After meditating on the timeliness of Jeanne Jugan's spiritual message, John Paul II brought to light the apostolic message, no less relevant, that she also left us.

"One could say that she received from the Holy Spirit what may be called a prophetic intuition of the needs and deep desires of the elderly.

Detail from an icon by George and Sergio Pinecross; Photo © Willy Berré.

Never having read or meditated upon the beautiful texts of *Gaudium et Spes*, Jeanne was already in secret harmony with what they say about establishing a great human family where all men are treated as brothers (n. 24), sharing the world's goods according to the law of justice which is inseparable from the law of charity (n.69) ... From the start, the foundress did not want her Congregation to limit itself to the west of France, but rather to become a real network of family-like homes where each person would be received, honored and even, to the extent possible to each one, brought to a new widening of his or her existence. The whole Church and society itself must admire and applaud the amazing growth of this little seed of the Gospel, sown in the soil of Brittany by that most humble woman of Cancale, so poor in possessions yet so rich in faith!"

"Live in admiration and thanksgiving on account of Blessed Jeanne Jugan, on account of her life, so humble and fruitful, which has truly become one of the numerous signs of God's presence in history." [2]

"Sign of the presence of God in human history." May this word of the Pope enlighten the journey of all those who have put their confidence in Jeanne Jugan, the humble Little Sister Mary of the Cross!

[2] John Paul II, during the audience on October 4, 1982 with the "pilgrims of Jeanne Jugan."

Beatification Homily
of Pope John Paul II
❧(October 3, 1982)❧

During the beatification ceremony representatives of Jeanne's native land present Pope John Paul II with a statue of St. Anne, the patroness of Brittany. Photo by L'Osservatore Romano.

And he lifted up the lowly! These well-known words of the Magnificat fill my spirit and my heart with joy and emotion after I have just declared the humble foundress of the Little Sisters of the Poor one of the Blessed. I give thanks to the Lord for bringing about what Pope John XXIII had so rightly hoped for and Paul VI so ardently desired. This text I have cited could surely be applied to the countless followers of Christ who have been beatified or canonized by the supreme authority of the Church. Nevertheless, a close reading of the Positio on the virtues of Jeanne Jugan, as well as of recent biographies about her and her epic of evangelical charity, inclines me to say that God could glorify no more humble a servant than she. Dear pilgrims, I have no fears about encouraging you to read or reread these works which speak so well of the heroic humility of Blessed Jeanne as well as of that wondrous divine wisdom which so carefully and patiently arranges events destined to help an exceptional vocation to flower and a new work to blossom, a work which is at once ecclesial and social.

Actuality of her spiritual message

Having said this, I would like to meditate with you, and for you, on the actuality of the spiritual message of the newly Blessed one. Jeanne invites all of us, and I quote here from the Rule of the Little Sisters, "to share in the beatitude of spiritual poverty, leading to that complete dispossession which commits a soul to God." She invites us to this much more by her life than by those few words of hers which have been recorded and which are so marked by the seal of the Holy Spirit, such as these: "It is so beautiful to be poor, to have nothing, to await all from God." Joyfully aware of her poverty, she depended completely on Divine Providence, which she saw operative in her own life and in that of others. Still, this absolute confidence did not make her inactive. With the courage and faith that characterizes the women of her native land, she did not hesitate to beg on behalf of the poor whom she cared for. She saw herself as their sister, their "Little Sister." She wanted to identify herself with all those elderly who were, often, more or less infirm and sometimes even abandoned. Is not this the Gospel in its pure form (cf. Mt. 25:35-41)? Is not this the way which the Third Order of Saint John Eudes had taught her: "to have one life, one heart, one soul, one will, with Jesus," to reach out to those whom Jesus had always preferred: the little ones and the poor? Thanks to her daily exercises of piety – long periods of silent prayer, participation in the Eucharistic Sacrifice and reception of Holy Communion more frequently than was the custom at that time, thoughtful recitation of the Rosary, which she had always with her, and fervent kneeling before the Stations of the Cross – the soul of Jeanne was steeped in the mystery of Christ the Redeemer, especially in his Passion and his Cross. Her name in religion, Sister Mary of the Cross, is a real and moving symbol of this. From her native village of Petites-Croix (in English, Little Crosses … was this a coincidence or a sign?) until her departure from this world on August 29, 1879, this foundress' life can be compared to a long and fruitful Way of the Cross, lived with a serenity and joy conformable to the Gospel. Must we not recall here that four years after the foundation of the Order, Jeanne was the victim of unjustifiable interference extraneous to the group of her first companions? She allowed herself to be stripped of the office of superior, and a little later on she accepted to return to the motherhouse for a retirement that was to last twenty-seven years, without the slightest complaint.

When summing up events such as these, the word "heroism" comes spontaneously to mind. Saint John Eudes, her spiritual master, used to say, "The real measure of sanctity is humility." By the fact of so often repeating to the novices, "Be little, stay little! Keep the spirit of humility, of littleness! If we begin to consider ourselves as something, the Congregation would no

Beatification tableau that hung in St. Peter's Basilica, by Dina Bellotti.

longer cause God to be honored and we would fall," Jeanne was really disclosing her own spiritual experience. In her long retirement at La Tour Saint Joseph, many novices and Little Sisters came under her decisive influence, and she left on her Congregation the stamp of her spirit by the quiet but eloquent radiance of her life. In our day, pride, the pursuit of efficacy, the temptation to use power, all run rampant, and sometimes, unfortunately, even in the Church. They become an obstacle

Mother General Marie Antoinette de la Trinité receives a blessing from Pope John Paul II during the Beatification festivities. Photo by L'Osservatore Romano.

to the coming of the Kingdom of God. This is why the spirituality of Jeanne Jugan can attract the followers of Christ and fill their hearts with simplicity and humility, with hope and evangelical joy having their source in God and in forgetfulness of self. Her spiritual message can lead all those baptized and confirmed to a rediscovery and a practice of that realistic charity which is stunningly effective in the life of a Little Sister or of a layperson when the God of Love and Mercy reigns there completely.

Actuality of her apostolic message

Likewise, Jeanne Jugan has left us an apostolic message most relevant for our day. You could say that she received from the Holy

Spirit what may be called a prophetic intuition of the needs and deep desires of the elderly: their desire to be respected, esteemed and loved; their fear of loneliness and at the same time their wish for a certain independence and privacy; their longing to still feel themselves useful; and very often, a strong desire to deepen their life of faith and to live it all the more. I would even add that, never having read the beautiful passages of "Gaudium et Spes," Jeanne was already in secret harmony with what they say about establishing a great human family where all men are treated as brothers (n. 24), sharing the world's goods according to the law of justice which is inseparable from the law of charity (n. 69). Though the structures of social security systems have done way with much of the misery of Jeanne Jugan's time, still her daughters come across great need among the elderly in many different countries today. And even where those structures do exist, they do not always provide the kind of home atmosphere the elderly so deeply desire and need for their physical and spiritual well-being. You can see it today: in a world where the number of older people is constantly growing, the timeliness of the apostolic message of Jeanne Jugan and her daughters cannot be disputed. From the start, the foundress did not want her Congregation to limit itself to the West of France, but rather to become a real network of family homes where each person would be received, honored and even, to the extent possible to each one, brought to a new widening of his or her existence. The timeliness of the apostolate undertaken by this foundress can be seen from the fact that there are today constant requests to be admitted to these homes and to found new ones. When she died, two thousand four hundred Little Sisters were ministering to the needs of the aged poor in ten countries. Today, there are four thousand four hundred of them in thirty nations and on six continents. The whole Church and society itself must admire and applaud the amazing growth of this little seed of the Gospel, sown in the soil of Brittany almost one hundred and fifty years ago by that most humble woman of Cancale, so poor in possessions yet so rich in faith.

May the beatification of their well-loved foundress impart to the Little Sisters of the Poor a new élan of fidelity to the spiritual and apostolic charism of their Mother! May the repercussions of this event, reaching to all the houses, have the effect of drawing more and more young women throughout the world into the ranks of the Little Sisters! May the glorification of their fellow countrywoman be a vigorous call to the parishioners of Cancale and the whole diocese of Rennes to the faith and love of the Gospel! Finally, may this beatification be a refreshing source of joy and of hope for all the aged of the world, thanks to the witness, hereby solemnly acknowledged, of the woman who loved all of them so much in the name of Jesus Christ and of his Church!

In a special audience following the beatification, Pope John Paul II greets Residents from around the world; here, with a group of French pilgrims, some dressed in traditional Breton costumes. Photo by L'Osservatore Romano.

Canonization Homily of Pope Benedict XVI

◈(St. Peter's Basilica, Sunday, October 11, 2009)◈

Excerpted from the Holy Father's homily at the canonization Mass for Saint Jeanne Jugan.

Postulators for Jeanne Jugan and the other four Servants of God canonized on October 11, 2009 stand before Pope Benedict XVI at the canonization Mass. Photo by L'Osservatore Romano.

By her admirable work at the service of the most deprived elderly, St. Mary of the Cross is also like a beacon to guide our societies which must always rediscover the place and the unique contribution of this period of life. Born in 1792 at Cancale in Brittany, Jeanne Jugan was concerned with the dignity of her brothers and sisters in humanity whom age had made more vulnerable, recognizing in them the Person of Christ himself. "Look upon the poor with compassion," she would say, "and Jesus will look kindly upon you on your last day". Jeanne Jugan focused upon the elderly a compassionate gaze drawn from her profound communion with God in her joyful, disinterested service, which she carried out with gentleness and humility of heart, desiring herself to be poor among the poor. Jeanne lived the mystery of love, peacefully accepting obscurity and self-emptying until her death. Her charism is ever timely while so many elderly people are suffering from numerous forms

A relic of Jeanne Jugan is carried in procession during the canonization ceremony. Photo by L'Osservatore Romano.

of poverty and solitude and are sometimes also abandoned by their families. In the Beatitudes Jeanne Jugan found the source of the spirit of hospitality and fraternal love, founded on unlimited trust in Providence, which illuminated her whole life. This evangelical dynamism is continued today across the world in the Congregation of Little Sisters of the Poor, which she founded and which testifies, after her example, to the mercy of God and the compassionate love of the Heart of Jesus for the lowliest. May St. Jeanne Jugan be for elderly people a living source of hope and for those who generously commit themselves to serving them, a powerful incentive to pursue and develop her work!

BIBLIOGRAPHY

Jeanne Jugan
Humble, So As To Love More
Paul Milcent, Translated by Alan Neame.
Darton, Longman and Todd, London, 1980, 230 pp. illustrated.

Poor in Spirit
Cardinal Gabriel-Marie Garrone, translated by Alan Neame.
Darton, Longman and Todd, 1975.
Published in the U.S.A. by Living Flame Press, 120 pp.

The Desert and the Rose
Eloi Leclerc, translated by Claire Trocmé.
Darton, Longman and Todd, 2002, 82 pp. illustrated.
Published in the U.S.A. as
Song of Silence, The Journey of Saint Jeanne Jugan.
Pauline Books and Media, 96 pp. illustrated.

Saint Jeanne Jugan: God's Tenderness for the World
Eloi Leclerc, translated by Patricia Kelly.
Darton, Longman and Todd, 2009, 64 pp. illustrated.

15 Days of Prayer with Saint Jeanne Jugan
Michel Lafon, translated by Louise Ashcroft.
New City Press, 140 pp.

Sayings of Jeanne Jugan
La Tour Saint Joseph, 1962-1981, 66 pp., illustrated.
Published in the U.S.A. by Little Sisters of the Poor Publications Office

At the Service of the Elderly
Jeanne Jugan and the Little Sisters of the Poor
René Berthier, Marie-Hélène Sigaut.
Translated by Charles Mann and the Little Sisters of the Poor.
Les Editions du Rameau. Illustrated story, 48 pp.

All materials on Jeanne Jugan are available in the United States
through the
Publications Office, 601 Maiden Choice Lane, Baltimore, MD 21228
www.littlesistersofthepoor.org

PRAYER
through the intercession of
JEANNE JUGAN

Jesus, You rejoiced and praised Your Father for having revealed to little ones the mysteries of the Kingdom of Heaven. We thank You for the graces granted to your humble servant, Jeanne Jugan, to whom we confide our petitions and needs.

Father of the Poor, you have never refused the prayer of the lowly. We ask You, therefore, to hear the petitions that she presents to You on our behalf.

Jesus, through Mary, Your Mother and ours, we ask this of You, who live and reign with the Father and the Holy Spirit now and forever.

Amen.

*Anyone receiving favors through the
intercession of Saint Jeanne Jugan is
asked to notify the nearest Home of the
Little Sisters of the Poor or their motherhouse:*

La Tour Saint Joseph
35190 Saint Pern
France